POCKET BOOK OF

HAPPINESS

First published in Great Britain 2020 by Trigger

Trigger is a trading style of Shaw Callaghan Ltd & Shaw Callaghan 23 USA, INC.

The Foundation Centre

Navigation House, 48 Millgate, Newark

Nottinghamshire NG24 4TS UK

www.triggerpublishing.com

Copyright © Trigger Publishing 2020

British Library Cataloguing-in-Publication data

A CIP catalogue record for this book is available upon request
from the British Library

ISBN: 9781789561852

Trigger Publishing has asserted their right under the Copyright,
Design and Patents Act 1988 to be identified as the author of this work

Cover design and typeset by Fusion Graphic Design Ltd.

Printed and bound in China by Hung Hing Printers Group Ltd.

Paper from responsible sources

POCKET BOOK OF

HAPPINESS

The mental health & wellbeing publisher

www.triggerpublishing.com

INTRODUCTION

Modern life can be filled with so much: from the daily commute, a hectic schedule and cooking an evening meal; to those crucial turning points: quitting your job, moving house, finding love. Between the noise, it can be hard to stop and recognise those all-important moments of joy.

The *Pocket Book of Happiness* offers a little guidance for when the scales of life are tipped, times become turbulent and a moment of reflection is needed. From the minds of some of the world's most well-known figures, learn to find your footing, take a breath and feel happy once more.

Don't ever underestimate the importance you
can have because history has shown
us that courage can be contagious and hope
can take on a life of its own

Michelle Obama

He who lives in harmony with himself
lives in harmony with the universe

Marcus Aurelius

But I know, somehow, that only when
it is dark enough can you see the stars

Martin Luther King Jr.

Doing what you like is freedom.
Liking what you do is happiness

Frank Tyger

"

I, not events, have the power to make me happy or unhappy today. I can choose which it shall be. Yesterday is dead, tomorrow hasn't arrived yet ...

... I have just one day, today,
and I'm going to be happy in it

Groucho Marx

You might not make it to the top, but if you are doing what you love, there is much more happiness there than being rich or famous

Tony Hawks

It's part of life to have obstacles.
It's about overcoming obstacles;
that's the key to happiness

Herbie Hancock

"

Our greatest happiness does not depend on the condition of life in which chance has placed us, but is always the result of a good conscience, good health ...

... occupation, and freedom
in all just pursuits

Thomas Jefferson

The pursuit of happiness is a most
ridiculous phrase: if you pursue happiness
you'll never find it

Carrie Snow

Happiness is secured through virtue;
it is a good attained by man's own will

Thomas Aquinas

Understanding your employee's perspective can go a long way towards increasing productivity and happiness

Kathryn Minshew

The greater part of our happiness
or misery depends on our dispositions
and not on our circumstances.
We carry the seeds of the one
or the other about with us in our
minds wherever we go

Martha Washington

Life is not a problem to be
solved but a reality to be experienced

Søren Kierkegaard

The moments of happiness we enjoy
take us by surprise. It is not that we seize
them, but that they seize us

Ashley Montagu

Nothing brings me more happiness
than trying to help the most vulnerable
people in society

Princess Diana

We all want to help one another. Human beings are like that. We want to live by each other's happiness, not by each other's misery

Charlie Chaplin

Action may not bring happiness but
there is no happiness without action

William James

There is no such thing as the pursuit of
happiness, but there is the discovery of joy

Joyce Grenfell

For every minute you are angry you
lose sixty seconds of happiness

Ralph Waldo Emerson

Happiness, not in another place
but this place ... not for another hour,
but this hour

Walt Whitman

“

Actions are right in proportion as they tend to promote happiness; wrong as they tend to produce the reverse of happiness ...

... By happiness is intended pleasure
and the absence of pain

John Stuart Mill

It's not possible to experience constant
euphoria, but if you're grateful,
you can find happiness in everything

Pharrell Williams

Folks are usually about as happy as they
make their minds up to be

Abraham Lincoln

Don't forget to tell yourself positive
things daily! You must love yourself
internally to glow externally

Hannah Bronfman

It's in responsibility that most people find the meaning that sustains them through life. It's not in happiness. It's not in impulsive pleasure

Jordan Peterson

In our lives, change is unavoidable,
loss is unavoidable. In the adaptability and
ease with which we experience change,
lies our happiness and freedom

Buddha

I don't have to take a trip around the world
or be on a yacht in the Mediterranean to have
happiness. I can find it in the little things,
like looking out into my backyard and
seeing deer in the fields

Queen Latifah

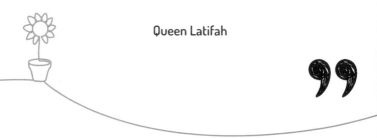

When you relinquish the desire to control your future, you can have more happiness

Nicole Kidman

Happiness is not doing fun things.
Happiness is doing meaningful things

Maxime Lagacé

If you aren't grateful for what you already have, what makes you think you would be happy with more

Roy T. Bennett

No matter what you're going through,
there's a light at the end of the tunnel and it
may seem hard to get to it but you can

Demi Lovato

"

My mother is a big believer in being
responsible for your own happiness.
She always talked about finding joy
in small moments ...

... and insisted that we stop and tak
in the beauty of an ordinary day

Jennifer Garner

Now and then it's good to pause in our pursuit of happiness and just be happy

Guillaume Apollinaire

It's the moments that I stopped just
to be, rather than do, that have
given me true happiness

Richard Branson

Stay positive and happy.
Work hard and don't give up hope.
Be open to criticism and keep learning ...

... Surround yourself with happy,
warm and genuine people

Tena Desae

I must learn to be content with
being happier than I deserve

Jane Austen

You cannot prevent the
birds of sadness from passing
over your head ...

... but you can prevent their
making a nest in your hair

Chinese proverb

Three grand essentials to happiness in this life are something to do, something to love, and something to hope for

Joseph Addison

Success is getting what you want.
Happiness is wanting what you get

Dale Carnegie

The most important thing is to
enjoy your life – to be happy
– it's all that matters

Audrey Hepburn

If you want to be happy,
set a goal that commands your thoughts,
liberates your energy and inspires your hopes

Andrew Carnegie

Do not anticipate trouble,
or worry about what may never happen

Benjamin Franklin

Happiness is when what you think,
what you say, and what you do
are in harmony

Mahatma Gandhi

Doing what you were born to do ...
that's the way to be happy

Agnes Martin

It is not how much we have, but how much we enjoy, that makes happiness

Charles Spurgeon

I am content; that is a blessing
greater than riches;
and he to whom that is given
need ask no more

Henry Fielding

The more grateful I am,
the more beauty I see

Mary Davis

Wine is constant proof that
God loves us and loves to see us happy

Benjamin Franklin

Happiness quite unshared can scarcely
be called happiness; it has no taste

Charlotte Brontë

All happiness depends on courage and work

Honoré de Balzac

The foolish man seeks happiness in the distance, the wise grows it under his feet

James Oppenheim

Being happy never goes out of fashion

Lilly Pulitzer

The mere sense of living is joy enough

Emily Dickinson

Happiness is a place between
too much and too little

Finnish proverb

"

Simplicity makes me happy

Alicia Keys

Happiness depends upon ourselves

Aristotle

"

The secret of health for
both mind and body is not
to mourn for the past,
worry about the future,
or anticipate troubles ...

... but to live in the present
moment wisely and earnestly

Buddha

There is only one happiness in this life,
to love and be loved

George Sand
(a.k.a. Amantine Lucile Aurore Dupin)

You're a happy fellow,
for you'll give happiness and joy to
many other people. There is nothing
better or greater than that!

Ludwig van Beethoven

"

Be happy for this moment.
This moment is your life

Omar Khayyam

I think everybody should get
rich and famous and do everything
they ever dreamed of ...

... so they can see that it's not the answer

Jim Carrey

Happiness is a gift and the trick is not to
expect it, but to delight in it when it comes

Charles Dickens

It is the very mark of the spirit of rebellion
to crave for happiness in this life

Henrik Ibsen

Happiness consists more in
conveniences of pleasure that
occur every day than in
great pieces of good fortune that
happen but seldom

Benjamin Franklin

Be happy with what you have and are,
be generous with both, and you
won't have to hunt for happiness

William E. Gladstone

There is no cosmetic for
beauty like happiness

Lady Blessington

It is difficult to find happiness
within oneself, but it is impossible
to find it anywhere else

Arthur Schopenhauer

Sometimes we don't find the thing
that will make us happy because we can't
give up the thing that was supposed to

Robert Brault

All life is an experiment.
The more experiments you
make the better

Ralph Waldo Emerson

The greatest happiness of life is
the conviction that we are loved;
loved for ourselves, or rather,
loved in spite of ourselves

Victor Hugo

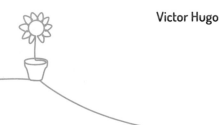

Spread love everywhere you go.
Let no one ever come without
leaving happier

Mother Teresa

You are responsible for your life.
You can't keep blaming somebody
else for your dysfunction.
Life is really about moving on

Oprah Winfrey

The happiness of life is made up of the
little charities of a kiss or smile, a kind look,
a heartfelt compliment

Samuel Taylor Coleridge

The habit of being happy enables
one to be freed, or largely freed, from the
domination of outward conditions

Robert Louis Stevenson

All happiness or unhappiness
solely depends upon the
quality of the object to which
we are attached by love

Baruch Spinoza

There is no happiness like that of
being loved by your fellow creatures,
and feeling that your presence
is an addition to their comfort

Charlotte Brontë

The most wasted of all days
is one without laughter

Nicolas Chamfort

Happiness is the best makeup

Drew Barrymore

Happiness is having a large,
loving, caring, close-knit family
in another city

George Burns

"

Even a happy life cannot be without a measure of darkness, and the word happy would lose its meaning if it were not balanced by sadness ...

... It is far better to take things as they come along with patience and equanimity

Carl Jung

The pain of parting is nothing
to the joy of meeting again

Charles Dickens

With freedom, books, flowers,
and the moon, who could not be happy

Oscar Wilde

Roll with the punches and enjoy
every minute of it

Meghan Markle, Duchess of Sussex

Man is fond of counting his troubles,
but he does not count his joys.
If he counted them up as he ought to
he would see that every lot
has enough happiness provided for it

Fyodor Dostoevsky

Don't waste a minute not being HAPPY.
If one window closes, run to the next
window or break down a door

Brooke Shields

The happiness of your life depends
upon the quality of your thoughts

Marcus Aurelius

With mirth and laughter let
old wrinkles come

William Shakespeare

66

If you want to be happy, be

Leo Tolstoy

Independence is happiness

Susan B. Anthony

"

I think the saddest people always
try their hardest to make people happy
because they know what it's like to
feel absolutely worthless ...

... and they don't want anyone
else to feel like that

Robin Williams

Most of us are just about as happy
as we make up our minds to be

William Adams

To be content means that you
realize you contain what you seek

Alan Cohen

The purpose of our lives is to be happy

Dalai Lama

If you can laugh, you can get through it

Jami Gertz

My family didn't have a lot of money,
and I'm grateful for that.
Money is the longest route to happiness

Evangeline Lilly

Real happiness is not of temporary
enjoyment, but is so interwoven with the
future that it blesses for ever

James Lendall Basford

True happiness is not attained
through self-gratification, but through
fidelity to a worthy purpose

Helen Keller

Blessed are those who can
give without remembering and take
without forgetting

Bernard Meltzer

We act as though comfort and luxury
were the chief requirements in life,
when all we need to make us really happy
is something to be enthusiastic about

Charles Kingsley

Success at the highest level comes down to one question: Can you decide that your happiness can come from someone else's success

Bill Walton

Happiness lies in the joy of achievement
and the thrill of creative effort

Franklin D. Roosevelt

The true secret of happiness lies in taking a genuine interest in all the details of daily life

William Morris

The worst part of success is trying to find someone who is happy for you

Bette Midler

Happiness can only be achieved
by looking inward & learning to enjoy
whatever life has and this requires
transforming greed into gratitude

Henry Fielding

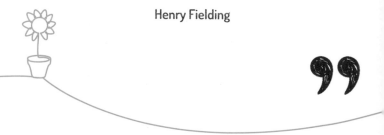

Happiness is where we find it,
but very rarely where we seek it

J. Petit Senn

Time you enjoy wasting
is not wasted time

Marthe Troly-Curtin

Optimism is a happiness magnet.
If you stay positive, good things and good
people will be drawn to you

Mary Lou Retton

The only thing that will make you
happy is being happy with who you are

Goldie Hawn

Be content with what you have;
rejoice in the way things are.
When you realize there is nothing lacking,
the whole world belongs to you

Lao Tzu

My happiness grows in direct proportion
to my acceptance, and in inverse
proportion to my expectations

Michael J. Fox

The talent for being happy is appreciating
and liking what you have,
instead of what you don't have

Woody Allen

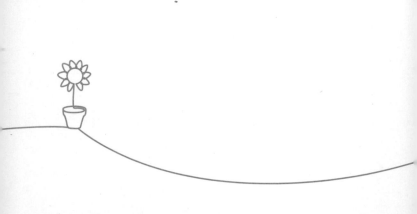

For a little guidance elsewhere ...

POCKET BOOK OF

FRIENDSHIP

For when life gets a little tough

POCKET BOOK OF

HOPE

For when life gets a little tough

TRIGGER™
The mental health & wellbeing publisher

www.triggerpublishing.com

We want to help you to not just survive
but thrive ... one book at a time

Find out more about Trigger Publishing by visiting our website:
triggerpublishing.com or join us on:

@TriggerPub

the *Shaw* mind
FOUNDATION

A proportion of profits from the sale of all Trigger
books go to their sister charity, The Shaw Mind Foundation,
founded by Adam Shaw and Lauren Callaghan.

The charity aims to ensure that everyone has access
to mental health resources whenever they need them.

Find out more: **shawmindfoundation.org** or join them on:

@Shaw_Mind   @ShawMindFoundation   @Shaw_Mind